T v Smith

Foruli Codex

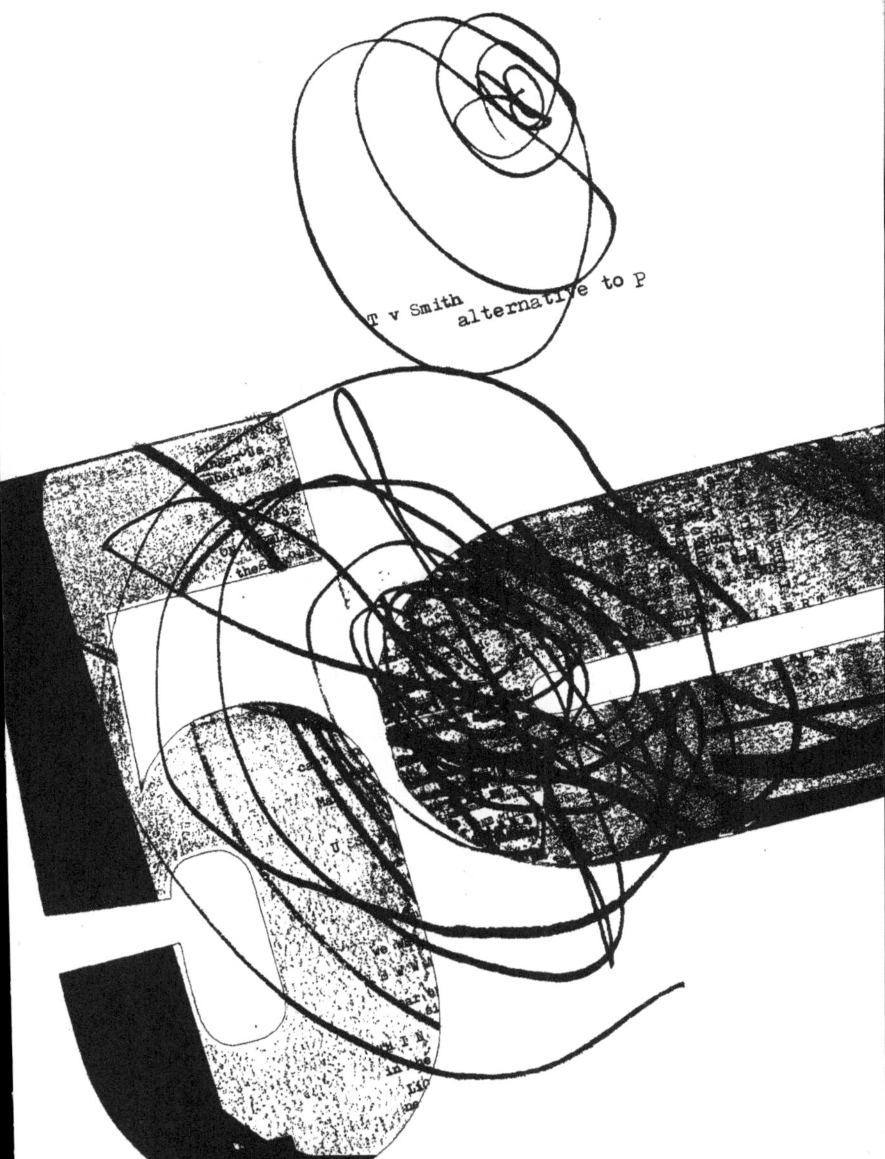

T v Smith alternative to P

Foruli Codex

Foruli Codex

Published by Foruli Codex

FIRST EDITION

ISBN 978-1-905792-68-9

Volume copyright © Foruli Ltd 2016
Cover design copyright © Foruli Ltd 2016
Foreword copyright © Henry Rollins 2016
All lyrics copyright © TV Smith

All lyrics reproduced by permission of the publisher.

Only One Flavour By Timothy Smith © HNKAKBSM Heike's Noch Kleinerer Aber Kein Bisschen Schlechterer Musikverlag. With kind permission of BMG Rights Management GmbH.

Tomahawk Cruise by kind permission of Rockin' Music.

Safety In Numbers, Great British Mistake, My Place, Bombsite Boy, On Wheels, Bored Teenagers, No Time To Be 21, We Who Wait, New Church, Cast Of Thousands, Television's Over, Gary Gilmore's Eyes, I Will Walk You Home reproduced by permission of Fire Songs.

Atlantic Tunnel, One Of Our Missiles, Ready For The Axe To Drop, The Day We Caught The Big Fish, Walk The Plank, Expensive Being Poor, Immortal Rich, Can't Pay Won't Pay, Useless, New Ways Are Best, March Of The Giants, Silicon Valley Holiday, Thin Green Line, Lion And The Lamb, Lord's Prayer, The Newshound, Borderline, Statute Of Liberty, Straight And Narrow published by Notting Hill Music (UK) Ltd.

Edited by Karl French

The right of TV Smith to be identified as the author of this work has been asserted by him in accordance with the Copyright, Designs and Patents Act 1988.

All rights reserved. No part of this publication may be reproduced, stored in or introduced into a retrieval system, or transmitted, in any form or by any means (electronic, mechanical, photocopying, recording or otherwise), without the prior written permission of the publisher. This book is sold subject to the condition that it shall not, by way of trade or otherwise, be lent, re-sold, hired out, or otherwise circulated without the publisher's prior written consent in any form of binding or cover other than that in which it is published and without a similar condition including this condition being imposed on the subsequent purchaser.

A CIP catalogue record for this book is available from the British Library

Design by Andy Vella, www.velladesign.com

Typeset in Vintage Vella Typewriter, a multitude of fonts, and scribbles

Printed by Lightning Source

Foruli Codex is an imprint of Foruli Ltd, London

www.forulicodex.com

alternative top 50

I'm always being asked it: what comes first, the words or the music? In fact they come together, mysteriously and intricately intertwined, an unholy alliance of message and melody.

So what happens when you pick them apart? There are the words, all naked without the music to disguise their true form. Released from the chains of verse-chorus-bridge they run free across the page, unexpected nuance and meaning exposed, shouting loud and proud their new purpose - no longer are we song, now we are poetry.

TV Smith, 2016

t v smith

1	PAGE 14	only one flavour
2	PAGE 16	clone town
3	PAGE 18	no t in my nam e
4	PAGE 20	GH OST of WESTMiNSTER
5	PAGE 22	gre at british mistake
6	PAGE 24	m y place
7	PAGE 26	atlanti c tunnel
8	PAGE 28	TOMAHAW k CRUISE
9	PAGE 30	one of our miseries
10	PAGE 32	dangerous playground
11	PAGE 34	bombsite boy
12	PAGE 36	probably
13	PAGE 38	ready for the axe to drop
14	PAGE 40	on wheels
15	PAGE 42	the day we caught the big fish
16	PAGE 44	walk the plank
17	PAGE 46	weak glu e
18	PAGE 48	expensive being poor
19	PAGE 50	immortal rich
20	PAGE 52	small rewards
21	PAGE 54	one million pounds
22	PAGE 56	worn once
23	PAGE 58	can't pay won't pay
24	PAGE 60	second class citizens

contents

alternative top 50

27	PAGE 66	bored teenagers
28	PAGE 68	no time to be 21
29	PAGE 70	the future used to be better
30	PAGE 72	we who wait
31	PAGE 74	new ways are best
32	PAGE 76	march of the giants
33	PAGE 78	silicon valley holiday
34	PAGE 80	thin green line
35	PAGE 82	in the arms of my enemy
36	PAGE 84	lion and the lamb
37	PAGE 86	new church
38	PAGE 88	lord's prayer
39	PAGE 90	true believers
40	PAGE 92	xmas bloody xmas
41	PAGE 94	good times are back
42	PAGE 96	cast of thousands
43	PAGE 98	the newshound
44	PAGE 100	television's over
45	PAGE 102	coming in to land
46	PAGE 104	borderline
47	PAGE 106	statute of liberty
48	PAGE 108	straight and narrow
49	PAGE 110	gary gilmore's eyes
50	PAGE 112	i will walk you home

t v smith

Henry Rollins

It is almost impossible to not somehow insinuate yourself into the story when you're writing about someone you greatly admire. I will have to apologise here right at the top for the next several lines. Please bear with.

In the late 1970s, when import singles started to make their way to the cooler record stores on the Eastern Seaboard of the United States, Ian MacKaye and I would often make a weekly trip to Yesterday & Today Records, owned by Skip Groff, to see what records had drifted in since our last visit.

It could have been one of our first visits to the store, and we were going through the singles bins when we saw a few Adverts records. We had read about the band and seen photos of them in Caroline Coon's book 1988: The New Wave Punk Rock Explosion, which turned out to be a very useful guide. We saw two copies of the 'Safety In Numbers'/'We Who Wait' single on Anchor Records. We both bought a copy.

8 foreword

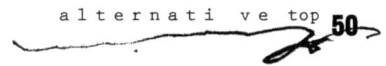

We got back to Ian's room and put the record on. 'Safety In Numbers' went searing into our brains for the first time. It wasn't a matter of 'What did he say?'

Here we all are in the latest craze
Stick with the crowd, hope it's not a passing phase
It's the latest thing to be nowhere
You can turn into the wallpaper
But you know you were always there anyway
Without the new wave

We heard TV Smith loud and clear on the first pass. I knew immediately that this was someone to pay very, very close attention to.

Soon after, we gathered every Adverts record we could find. With each listen, the lyrics only seemed to become more insightful and, dare I say, hell, I dare—profound.

Not only was TV Smith not buying into the stimulant-fuelled, often wilfully generated stupidity in the scene – wasn't Punk Rock trying to get away from the ten million miles of dull, cattle-call music that, thankfully, irritated just the right people who created this new music in the first place, as if expressing yourself below your intellectual pay grade was to be in any way admired? – his lyrics assessed what was happening at the time and what was coming.

TV Smith's unflinching, lidless, laser-directed eye was the keenest blade in the arsenal. When anyone would say, 'Punk Rock is stupid,' all you had to do was play this person an Adverts song and even the harshest critic had to admit, *That was, wow, completely spot-on.*

Have you ever bought one record after another in the almost naïve hope that, if you searched long enough, you would find the song you had been waiting to hear all your life, a song that perfectly summed up your existence at that point? A rather weathered copy of what ended up being one of the last Adverts singles arrived at the record store, and within hours was on the turntable. I had found the song.

9

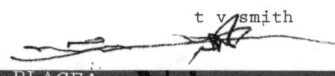

t v smith

'MY PLACE'

Some God must have spewed me up

I lie in the street until the sun comes up

When I come to my senses again

I survey the waste

Here it is

All around me

My place

From writers to scientists

It's all the same - more facts to twist

I've been hit by passing fists

But this is where I'll stay

Here it is

All around me

My place

Throw the shroud on modern times

Touch my lips with spiced wine

On the ropes I live on hope

Of better days

Here it is

All around me

My place

Never let me forget that

I'm staying here in my place

alternative top **50**

After what was one of the best sophomore album efforts in all of Punk Rock, with lyrics so concentrated and well-crafted you imagined TV had somehow put his DNA into a vice to extract them, *Cast Of Thousands* was the last official full-length release of the Adverts.

It was right after the Adverts signed off that we learned something key to understanding the modus operandi of TV Smith, which holds to this day: TV is a fully-committed, full-time songwriter and performer. No trend or bend in the world of music or the world-at-large will deter him. Without so much as a pause, TV was already hard at work with his next group, TV Smith's Explorers, and if anything, his blade was only getting sharper.

In his first post-Adverts track with the Explorers, TV speaks of an ordnance delivery system that will become so commonly used, horrific human fatalities now read like a weather report. Rather than to merely list what can happen and what the cost will be, TV Smith's artistry shows brilliantly as he actually takes on the mind-set of a Tomahawk missile, cool and removed, only dangerous when utilised by the weapon's taskmaster. TV's almost resigned posture brings home the true terror of a missile attack: you can be killed by a stranger from a great distance with the push of a button. From 'Tomahawk Cruise':

If you so wish I could get nasty
Create all kinds of disasters
I know things run away with you
But at the cusp you have to choose
Between living and Tomahawk Cruise

This was, if you will, only the warm-up. There was so much more to come.

There was a treacherous era for many musicians, no doubt you remember. This was a time that causes some of the best artists to look back and cringe at several aspects of their output, from some of the choices in production to hairstyles and videos. Some of it is absolutely cringeful and you have to feel some sympathy: there was obviously something going 'round and a lot of people came down with it. It was called The 1980s. It was a wave of awful that TV survived unscathed, wrapping up operations with the Explorers, then releasing the very good *Channel Five* album, and finishing out

the decade with his next line-up, Cheap. These songs are quite good, and as always, the lyrics are those of a man who refuses to turn away from what is.

The 1990s were even better. One of his career standout albums, *The Immortal Rich*, seemed to push him forward into some of his finest work, which informs what he is currently doing.

This is not supposed to be a biography but it is next to impossible to speak of TV Smith's output without some chronological reference because there isn't a time period where TV went quiet. Some periods are more prolific than others – that's how it goes – but there is rarely a period where there wasn't a release or a tour with new material.

TV Smith is a lifer, a man with a guitar who goes into what Mark Twain referred to as 'the territory' and brings the good gear, year after year. This is by no means unique. There are a lot of people who tread the boards decade after decade but quite often they have long ago lapsed into parody and don't mind being a cartoon of themselves if it pays the rent. Thankfully, this is not the story of TV Smith. The proof is all those great records that keep coming out and the full commitment to relentless touring. At the time of this writing, I Delete is TV's newest album. It is damn good and has the energy and intensity of someone half his age.

It is fair to associate TV Smith with what we call Punk Rock. It is not a pejorative term when applied to the man. That being said, for a bunch of anarchists, drunks, and otherwise anti-structuralists, there were some ground rules, even though they may have been written on a beach at low tide. This music was supposed to cut through. It's not that it couldn't be tuneful or even fun but it had to have at least a modicum of substance, otherwise we could all go back to the boomy arenas and watch bands from a great distance as they distractedly dialled in yet another tired rendition of themselves.

As far as what came before Punk, it wasn't broken but did it need breaking? Actually, music, culture, expectation, what is considered 'how it is' all need to be constantly challenged and 'broken' from time to time. This is where Punk Rock the genre can sometimes disappoint. To a certain extent it lost its ability to warn, to inform and to provide counterpoint.

alternative top 50

At least one person from 'back in the day' never lost the plot, never came in from the cold for the poison-laced prize of commercial acceptance, never lapsed into pathetic caricature, never stopped looking at it and really seeing it, and not only that, rendering these scalpel-sharp observations in astonishingly great verse. Some, not all mind you, but some of his lyrics are in this book.

Oh, and as a postscript, here is a recent communiqué from TV to me that says it all:

I just finished a cool gig in front of 65 people in a little town near the Ramstein airbase in Germany. Good people.
Cheers, Tim

HENRY ROLLINS. 2016

t v smith

I

14 only one flavour

alternative top 50

This is how it starts up
A slap and a cry
The slaps keep coming
For the rest of your life
And you don't know who to question
And you don't know how to fight
You just hope that by the end
It turns out alright

There's only one flavour
Only one way to go

No opposition
Only one view to hold

I weathered out those anxious years
Of boom and slump
In a tree and a tunnel and a tent
And a truck by a garbage dump
My life was like a motorway
My wheels were square
Sometimes I wonder
How I got anywhere
There's only one flavour
Only one way to go
A single direction
Only one face to show

Every crank, poet, genius
Pressured off the devious
Tied to the coat-tails
Speeding down the monorail

I woke up and I was driving
There was blood on my hands
I felt like a stranger
In an over-familiar land
Well, we all fall to the centre
But my eyes are full of stars
Sometimes I wonder
How I ever got this far
There's only one flavour
Only one way to go
No opposition
Only one view to hold
A single direction
Only one truth to know

t v smith

alternative top 50

IT'S A CHAIN STORE MASSACRE
BODIES LYING EVERYWHERE
THOSE WITH THE BIGGEST CLOUT
PUNCH THE INDEPENDENTS OUT
WE'RE SPIED ON, HERDED ROUND
STRANDED ON THE UNDERGROUND
ABANDONED WITH OUR HAPPY MEAL
INSIDE A RING OF STEEL
IT'S DISTURBING
BUT IT'S WORKING
I DON'T FIT IN
TO A CLONE TOWN

WHERE THE FACELESS, TASTELESS
GET RICH QUICK
WE'RE TOO BUSY SHOPPING
TO NOTICE THE APOCALYPSE
FUMING IN THE RAT RUNS
NO ONE'S HAVING ANY FUN
THE STREETS ARE PAVED WITH CHEWING GUM
MY MIND IS GOING NUMB
IT'S DISTURBING
BUT IT'S WORKING
I DON'T FIT IN
TO A CLONE TOWN

WHERE ALL WE KNOW IS WHAT THEY TELL US
NOTHING SLIPPING THROUGH THE CENSORS
MANUFACTURED SATISFACTION
WAR REDUCED TO PURE ABSTRACTION
TOO CONFUSED TO TAKE A STAND
IMPRISONED IN A PROMISED LAND
PREDICTABLE, REPETITIVE AND BLAND
BUT DO YOU REALLY WANT TO KNOW
HOW THEY GET THOSE PRICES SO LOW?
IT'S DISTURBING
BUT IT'S WORKING
I DON'T FIT IN
TO A CLONE TOWN

t v smith

1 2
  3

18   no t   in my   nam e

alternative top 50

Why should I have to show my I.D.
There's no consensus and I don't agree
With what they're undertaking in my name
I'm appalled and I'm ashamed

Why should I have to show my I.D.
To be enrolled in this community
Where all my role models are on the take
And the real thing is fake
All my heroes died
While they were still alive
Confused or compromised
Their values undermined
They were led down to the hole
Where the blood money flows

Why should I have to show my I.D.
Someone somewhere's got a file on me
Someone somewhere's got a file on you
Anyone will do

The world's ruled by the elite
Cheats and gangs of thieves
Whose lies and double-speak
Spread faster than disease
And your pursuit of peace
Will mark you out a freak
A victim and a bore
While their portfolios soar
And weapons sales will peak
Aimed only at the weak
Those already on their knees
It's arms for amputees
It's the bullet's exit hole
Where the blood money flows
Never again!
Not in my name!

Bad guys come first
The third world thirsts,
Starves, or dies of AIDS
In the modern day crusades
The Wild West will win
Defeat the Indians
Drive the devils to the door
With the homeless and the poor
And when there's nothing left to bomb
No-one left to beat

They'll train their cross wires on
The unseen enemy
The ever-present threat
That hasn't happened yet
And probably never will
Still they move in for the kill
But the night sights won't show
If you're friend or foe
Are you so much better than
The junkies and Saddam?
Are you guaranteed a place
When they build the master race?
Will the world then be pure?
We've heard that one before
In history's deepest holes
Where the blood money flowed
Never again!
Not in my name!

t v smith

1 2 4
 3

GHO ST

of WESTMiNSTER

alternative top 50

THE LIGHTS HAVE BEEN SWITCHED OUT
THE PARTY'S OVER
THE GUESTS HAVE ALL GONE HOME
NOW IN THESE SILENT HOURS
THAT THE NIGHT DEVOURS
THROUGH THE HALLOWED HALLS I ROAM
ONCE I WAS JUST LIKE YOU
SUBSTANTIAL, WHOLE AND TRUE
ABLE TO INFLUENCE
THE PASSAGE OF EVENTS
WE LINED UP FACE TO FACE
STOOD TWO SWORD LENGTHS APART
I RAN THE GAUNTLET
AND THEY STABBED ME THROUGH THE HEART
THE WORLD WENT COLD
NOW I'M THE GHOST OF WESTMINSTER

HOW THEY MUST HATE THAT WHEEL
SO CHILD-LIKE AND UNREAL
THAT MOCKS THEIR CONSTITUTION
WITH EACH REVOLUTION
LAWS LAID DOWN THROUGH THE YEARS
PROCEDURE AND DEBATE
THE WITCHCRAFT OF MY PEERS
THAT LEFT ME IN THIS STATE
THE GHOST OF WESTMINSTER

SO I AM CONDEMNED
TO WALK BESIDE THE STINKING THAMES
FORGOTTEN BY MY FORMER FRIENDS
WHO WAVE THEIR PAPERS AND ANNOUNCE
THE SPIRIT HAS BEEN DRIVEN OUT
AND NEVER MORE WILL HAUNT THIS HOUSE
BUT THROUGH THE HOLLOW NIGHT
I HOLD ON TO THE HOPE
THAT I AM STILL ALIVE
AND REALLY THEY'RE THE GHOSTS
OF WESTMINSTER

t v smith

1 2 4
 3 5

22 gre at british mistake

alternati ve top **50**

The Great British Mistake was looking for a way out - was getting complacent - not noticing the pulse was racing - the mistake was fighting the change - was staying the same - it couldn't adapt so it couldn't survive - something had to give - the people take a downhill slide into the gloom - into the dark recesses of their minds

                I swoop over your city like a bird

                I climb the high branches and observe

                Into the mouth

        Into the soul

    I cast a shadow

That swallows you whole

I swoop

I climb

I cling

I swallow you whole

String out the drip-feed - they're losing their world - they're losing their hard boys and magazine girls - advert illegal - TV as outlaw - motive as spell - they'll see the books burn - they'll be 451 - it's people against things and not against each other - out of the pre-pack - into the fear - into themselves - they're the Great British Mistake - the genie's out of the bottle - call in the magician - they didn't mean to free him - devil behind them - devil in the mirror - chained to their right hand - they're the Great British Mistake - they have to come to terms now - they'll take it out somehow - blame it all on something - the British Mistake - when will it be over - how can they avoid it?

t v smith

1 2   4
   3 5
      6

24 m y place

alternative top 50

SOME GOD MUST HAVE SPEWED ME UP
I LIE IN THE STREET UNTIL THE SUN COMES UP
WHEN I COME TO MY SENSES AGAIN
I SURVEY THE WASTE
HERE IT IS
ALL AROUND ME
MY PLACE

FROM WRITERS TO SCIENTISTS
IT'S ALL THE SAME - MORE FACTS TO TWIST
I'VE BEEN HIT BY PASSING FISTS
BUT THIS IS WHERE I'LL STAY
HERE IT IS
ALL AROUND ME
MY PLACE

THROW THE SHROUD ON MODERN TIMES
TOUCH MY LIPS WITH SPICED WINE
ON THE ROPES I LIVE ON HOPE
OF BETTER DAYS
HERE IT IS
ALL AROUND ME
MY PLACE
NEVER LET ME FORGET THAT
I'M STAYING HERE IN MY PLACE

t v smith

1 2 4
  3 5
   6 7

26 atlanti c tunnel

alternative top **50**

Far beneath those sunken ships
We've got muscle-bound workers
And scientists
And some of them are working
Twenty-four hour shifts
Because the whole world's waiting for this
Atlantic tunnel
Coming straight to you
Smashing through the bedrock
And the culture shock
With a boom, boom, boom

From the land of the roller skate
It's the same great team
Who put a man in space
With a new flavour bubble gum
You have to taste
It's like a bomb blowing up in your face
Atlantic tunnel
Coming straight to you
Breaking bones of dinosaurs
On the ocean floors
With a boom, boom, boom

I name this tunnel *Mayflower 2*
And it's coming at you
Like a long lasso
Who cares?
Why kick up a fuss?
We need a satellite state
That thinks the same as us
We want to smoke your peace pipe
And abuse your trust
There's a whole world
Waiting to cross
Atlantic tunnel
Coming straight to you
Smashing through the bedrock
With the aftershocks
Going boom, boom, boom

t v smith

1 2 4
  3 5
    6 7
      8

alternative top 50

I woke up this morning, felt completely at ease
Put on some clothes and had something to eat
No desire to act, no desire to move
Unless I get a reason from you
My name is Tomahawk Cruise

We will our problems, we will our fate
But we have to eat what we put on the plate
Some people wallow in hate, some wallow in fear
Neither of the two are recommended round here

If you so wish I could get nasty
Create all kind of disasters
I know things run away with you
But at the cusp you have to choose
Between living and Tomahawk Cruise

Now in my heart something starts
Down in my heart something starts

I get your message, I understand
Break down the barriers as fast as you can
I dream unnatural power, unnatural grace
Bricks and wreckage all over the place
I change my clothes for a uniform
Throw caution to the wind and walk into the storm
At the cusp you choose
Between living and Tomahawk Cruise

I look at myself
What is this body?
A few limbs, stock responses
A heart turned to steel
I just love the attention
I'm in the news!

t v smith

```
  2
I   4   9
 3 5
   6 7
     8
```

30 one of our missiles

alternative top 50

We can link hands around the world
We can cross continents with a telephone cable
Now when the voice of progress calls
It sounds like it's just next door
New York beams the big fight to our satellite
And we can see it in England in the middle of the night
We can find deposits of minerals
Track down criminals
Find the proverbial needle
And lost tribes in the jungle
We can read your front page from a thousand miles up
Discover just about everything
But uh-oh
I'm afraid that
One of our missiles is missing
It vanished into thin air
Now it could be anywhere

Life's full of ups and downs
Usually we can even them out
Usually you're safe in our hands
Usually nothing happens
Most of the time things go as planned
Most of the time we're in command
Well, this is just our luck
Most things don't matter much
But uh-oh
I'm afraid that
One of our missiles is missing
It vanished into thin air
Now it could be anywhere
One of our missiles is missing
Oh, don't make such a fuss
It's bound to turn up

```
      2      4       10
 1       5     9  .
   3
       6 7
          8
```

32 dangerous playground

alternative top 50

If this is all there is

It's not enough

So many toys to play with

But you have to grow up

So many roads to go down

Which one will you choose?

The one that leads you to yourself

Or somewhere else?

You only know you have to go

You'll go because you must

I hope you find the things you lack

It's never enough

I left my home
I left my friends
I took the road that never ends
I left my roots
Took to my heels
Went on my way
I found the heat
I found the dust
Where even innocence gets lost
I found a place
Where games could never be
The same again
A dangerous playground

Tattered flags
Body bags
A sense of threat
A world of hate
Where every step
Could be the last one
I would take
Helicopters overhead
The stench of death
Children wept
I found a place
Where games could never be
The same again
A dangerous playground
The toys are all broken
Game over
There's no going home
My eyes have been opened

t v smith

$1 \quad {}^2_3 \quad {}^4_5 \quad {}_6{}^7_8 \quad 9\,{}^{10}\!{}_{11}$

34 bombsite boy

Leapfrog over fences
Little time, less senses
Here by this railway cutting
Life goes quick and it goes without warning
That's how life is in my bombsite dwelling

But I don't believe you have to be an idiot
To get somewhere these days
I don't believe you have to sell your soul
And do what everybody says
Or get carried away
Nowadays I fall among the empty shells and pray
Give thanks, I'm happy where I am - it's just as well
Well, I thank God I never closed my eyes
Thank God I never compromised
Thank God I wasn't mesmerised
The bombsite boy

There's a killer in your subway
An anarchist on your street
There's a breakdown on your T.V.
You can't find no relief
In fact no feelings at all
Your war is totally internal
At least I'm sure that mine is on the outside

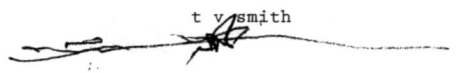

1   2   4   10 11
      3   5   9   12
          6 7
            8

probably

alternative top 50

All night spent at the circus
At the end you still have to bow down
Before the clowns
Even though the mean streets have been purged
And we laugh at danger now
Stick around
Who let the lions out of their cages?
Like laughter, fear is contagious

I heard a joke, my guardian angels
Are really total strangers
Who track my moves
Every aberration is frowned on
The searchlight shines down
On those who choose
To break the rules
Well, some of us make 'em
Some of us break 'em
Excuse me, but if I'm not mistaken
Probably
We're probably as safe as we'll ever be
Because the world is wild and free
And there is no certainty
So probably you're better off taking a ride with me
At least it breaks the monotony
Probably

Even though we're bored and sedated
There's a chance we could get creative
There's a chance we'll rise up and look down
Upon the clowns
Ever since I joined that trapeze act
My feet haven't touched the ground
And now probably
We're probably as safe as we'll ever be
Because the world is wild and free
And there is no certainty
And probably
There's probably more than the eye can see
To this state of security
Probably
And probably they're exploiting our vulnerability
And our need for stability
To force us into compliancy
So probably you're better off taking a ride with me
To an unknown destiny
At least it breaks the monotony
Probably

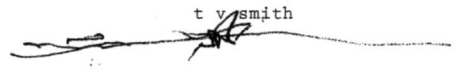
t v smith

1 2   4   10 11
   3 5   9   12
      6 7   13
        8

38 ready for the axe to drop

alternative top 50

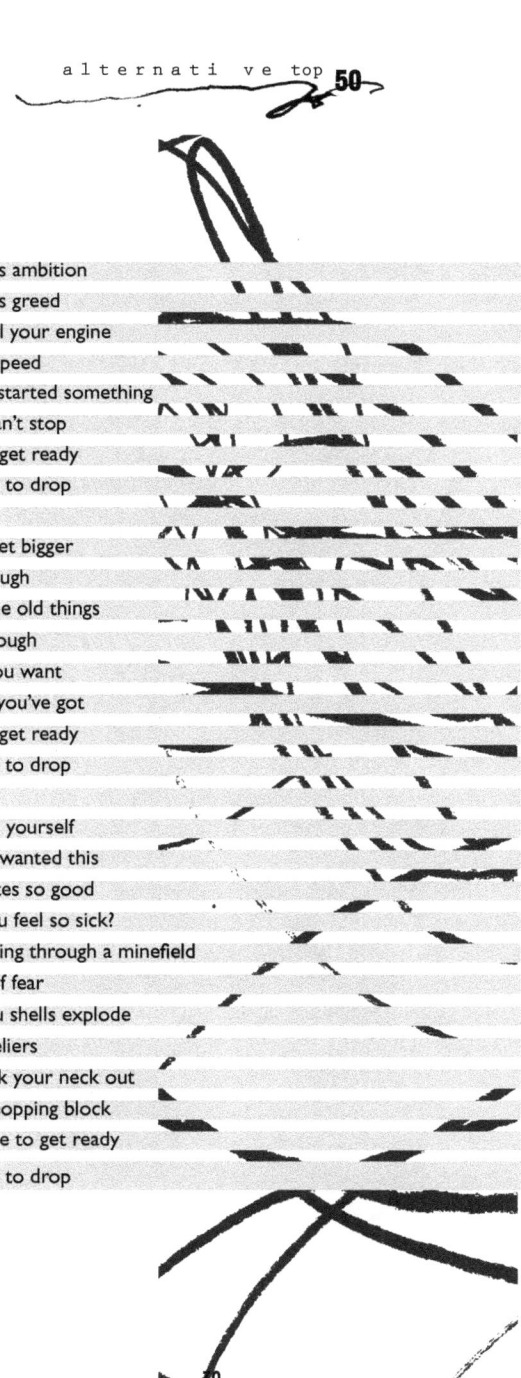

Here comes ambition
Here comes greed
You can feel your engine
Get up to speed
But you've started something
That you can't stop
It's time to get ready
For the axe to drop

Your toys get bigger
Play gets rough
Suddenly the old things
Are not enough
Suddenly you want
More than you've got
It's time to get ready
For the axe to drop

You can tell yourself
You always wanted this
But if it tastes so good
Why do you feel so sick?
You're walking through a minefield
Heart full of fear
Around you shells explode
Like chandeliers
You've stuck your neck out
Across a chopping block
And it's time to get ready
For the axe to drop

1 2   4   10 11
   3   5   9 12 14
       6 7   13
         8

40 on wheels

alternative top **50**

What's
left in the wheelchair
Who bothers what's in there
Who worries what life's like
On wheels

No body to speak of
No willpower, voice, love
Who intends to steer us
On wheels

I'm some new kind of great explorer
I sink the lowest, I go further
I'm sailing on the Lucky Dragon
I'm ready for whatever happens
Living out the life unstable
Men like animals, untameable
On wheels

What's left in the wheelchair
A taste of life and death together
I wish this embrace could last forever
On wheels

t v smith

```
          10
 2     4    11
1   4 5  9
  3  6 7  12 14
      8    13 15
```

42 the day we caught the big fish

alternative top 50

They called me skipper
And I sailed on the sea
Home was the rolling waves
And the beer and the company
And we pulled the nets together
And we worked as a team
Until the day we caught the big fish
And were never seen again

And the clock kept ticking
And my supper went cold
On the day we caught the big fish
And my wife was widowed

We'd talk of the old days
That would never come back
When we needed those muscles
Just to haul in the catch
When the ropes were singing
And our skins grew brown
On the day we caught the big fish
It was all hands down

And the boats kept searching
There was no trace found
On the day we caught the big fish
It was all hands down

When I hit the water
I was still laughing at a joke
That was just done telling
When the monster awoke
And I thought of all the legends
As I heard the winches scream
Then I swam with the Devil
In the deep blue sea

And the clock kept ticking
And my supper went cold
There were radio messages
That they couldn't decode
So the boats kept searching
There was no trace found
On the day we caught the big fish
It was all hands down

t v smith

```
          10
  2    4    11
1    5  9
  3  6 7 12 14
      8  1315
            16
```

44 walk the plank

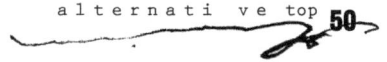

          The whole family sleeps here
Six to a room
My wife threads a needle
I push a broom
And dream of a hallway
Leading to a light
Five in the morning
I wake up tired
And they say
Walk the plank
We need you to
Walk the plank
So we don't have to

Parts of this city
I daren't show my face
Still the poor relation
Some call me 'ape'
Unrest and violence
Crime and drugs
Breed in the dark places
Where they abandoned us
And they say
Walk the plank
Because we blame you
Walk the plank
So we don't have to

The cost of living's falling
Not for us
Pay is rising
But the differential's up
I dream of a hallway
In a house of kings
Fly to my ancestors
On golden wings
      Up there I wear a crown
           Here I'm a slave
                Used to divert attention
                    While the thieves escape

t v smith

```
             10
   2    4  9  11
1    5    12  14
 3  6 7   13 15
     8       16
             17
```

46 weak glu e

alternative top **50**

This trail of blame
It's hard to follow
We clench our teeth
And swallow
When the levee breaks
The dregs of this human race
Float to the surface
No help comes through
Held together with weak glue
You're scared?
Me too
Held together with weak glue

In this calm oasis
Where violence rages
We hate our neighbours
Fight for parking spaces
This close to anarchy
It's all we can do to keep
Our heads above water
We split in two
Held together with weak glue
You're scared?
Me too
Held together with weak glue

No help came through
No aid, no food
Just TV crews
You're scared?
Me too
Held together with weak glue

We needed help
The troops were somewhere else
Are we so worthless?

t v smith

```
  2      10
1    4  9  11
  3 5   12  14
   6 7    1315
     8       16
            17 18
```

48 expensive being poor

alternative top 50

And the car is off the road
But I never had a car
And I pay more for my food
Because the supermarket's too far
It's expensive being poor
Because everything costs more
Knocking on a closing door
It's expensive being poor
Someone throw me down some crumbs
I will eat them off the floor
It's expensive being poor
But I look good when I get desperate

And the box is on the fritz
It's a black and white, or was
I tried taking it to bits
Now the picture's just a grey fuzz
It's expensive being poor
Because everything costs more
Someone pick me off the floor
It's expensive being poor
How can I live with what I did
When the cinema's six quid?
It's expensive being poor
But I look good when I get desperate

Let the good times roll
Into a bottomless hole
With job, friends and future
My ideal home furniture
Let the trumpets sound
As my house falls down

And the dust begins to clear
And I'm lying on the ground
And I'm standing on a path
In an unknown part of town
And the path leads me away
Over hills and out of sight
In the blazing sun by day
And the hanging moon by night
And I wind up in a place
Where I never have to count
And I never see the waves
As I push my leaking boat out
It's expensive being poor
Because everything hurts more
Knocking on a bolted door
It's expensive being poor
Someone throw me down some crumbs
I will eat them off the floor
It's expensive being poor
But I look good when I get desperate

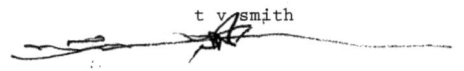

19

```
      2       10
 1       4  9   11
    3   5   12  14
       6 7     13 15
          8       16
                17  18
```

50   immortal rich

alternative top 50

I ate a suicide breakfast
And I still feel sick
I've got a half-life here
And I'm stuck with it
But I count my blessings
And say my prayers
Because half the world's hungry
And most of it's scared
And it's a cruel law
But the cat gets the cream
Cash buys the diet
Fit for a king
While the lion goes to the water hole
We must sit and wait
But any day now
We may scratch that itch
And join the immortal rich

They've got a drive-in Jesus
To purge their sins
Roll up to the gates of heaven
And still get in
Well, a big donation
Ain't going to hurt
And you get your name
On the TV church
Meanwhile down here
We've lost our faith
Look to the heavens
And just see rain
Can't meet the subscription
On the pray-to-pray
So we don't even watch

Death by a thousand cuts
Jack up the prices
So they cost
Just that much more
Than we can ever afford
Clean up in the hospitals
Close down all the wards
And it's a cruel law
But the cat gets the cream
Cash buys the lifestyle
Fit for a king
While the big cars
Ease into the fast lane
We come to a stop

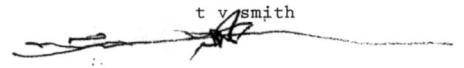

    19

1 2   4   10
   3 5   9   11
      6 7 12 14
         8 1315
              16 20
              17 18

52 small rewards

alternative top 50

Hard lines are all we hold
Truth is never told
In this misinformation overload
Where waves of groundless panic
Engulf the planet
We barricade the door
And are thankful for
Small rewards

Millions are suffering
But tonight let's order in
And watch the happy stuff
Is that enough?
This mindless entertainment
It's damage limitation
What keeps us tuning in?
All they are offering is
Small rewards

Yes, it starts small
But soon you're hooked
By their loving looks
While behind the scene
They cook the books
The best price is not on eBay
Head out, find the freeway
And enjoy the ride
Why be satisfied with
Small rewards?

19

```
                10
  2       9      11
1   4   5     12  14
  3  6 7    1315
       8      16  20   21
              17 18
```

54 one million pounds

alternative top 50

I couldn't tell my remote control from my phone
Deep in the mainstream I still felt alone
I only wanted to see the light
But I was looking right
At the darkness
In the bottom
Of the hole
One million pounds
Wouldn't turn this car around
One million pounds
In my pocket
I'd turn it down

I backed off from the blandishments and the bribes
Peeled away the blindfold covering my eyes
I'd been kneeling down to a tin god
Paid in pennies for a dirty job
They can keep it
Now I'm going
For a ride

Tried out
Found wanting
Worthless
Thrown aside
Passed by
Left for dead
But if you scratch off the surface you see the gold
Respond to the urging deep in your soul
I'm going to drive out in the dead of night
Through the roadblocks and red traffic lights
I don't know where I will end up
But I know
One million pounds
Wouldn't turn this car around
One million pounds
Worth of nothing
I'd turn it down

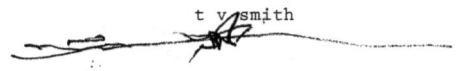

.19

```
   2       10
1    4   9   11
  3  5    12 14
   6 7   1315     21
      8     16 20 22
            17 18
```

56 worn once

alternative top 50

SHATTERED STREETS, SHATTERED TOWN
BOARDED UP, SHUTTERED DOWN
BAD LOANS, BROKEN HOMES
THEN A PHOENIX ARISES
POURING SCORN ON THE CRISIS
THERE'S CREDIT
WE'RE READY, LET'S JUMP
BUT THE THINGS YOU RELY ON
AREN'T LIKE CLOTHES YOU JUST TRY ON
THEN DISPOSE OF
WORN ONCE

SHATTERED DREAMS, SHATTERED LIVES
EASILY SATISFIED
IF YOU BELIEVE THE PUBLICITY
AN INSTANT HIGH IS ALL YOU NEED
YOU CAN SPEND WITHOUT THINKING
BUT THE SHIP IS STILL SINKING
AND YOU KNOW WHEN IT COMES TO THE CRUNCH
THAT THE THINGS YOU RELY ON
AREN'T LIKE CLOTHES YOU JUST TRY ON
THEN DISPOSE OF
WORN ONCE

COLD CALLS, STORE WARS
THEY'LL GIVE YOU SOMETHING FOR NOTHING
BEST BUYS, STAR PRIZE
BUT THE LOWER THE PRICES
THE MORE COMPROMISES
YOU CAN'T SHRUG OFF
WORN ONCE
THESE THROWAWAY VALUES
THEY WILL HOLD YOU
THEN HAVE YOU
DISPOSED OF
WORN ONCE

.19

```
    2    4    10
 1    5    9  11
   3 6   12 14
     7 8 1315    21
          16 20 22
           17 18  23
```

58 can't pay won't pay

alternative top 50

* * * * * *   *   *

They bought a rocket
They bought a nuclear submarine
They're playing war games
In the snow and mud
With a white flag flying
They put a blood red bill in my hands
It's nothing to do with me
I can't pay
And I won't pay
For their mistakes

They're generating
While the waves come rolling in
Pumping black smoke
From their chimney stacks
While the world tries to turn green
I get the cost of the clean up
It's nothing to do with me
I can't pay
And I won't pay
For their mistakes

I'm underneath their table
Picking up their scraps
Nobody knows where the money goes
They set a tax then another tax
But it must be democratic
Because I let them do it to me
I watch the fat cats get fatter
While I stay lean
In this free market
What's happening?
I've got questions
Objections
Has this fast food travelled at the speed of greed
From the space race to my tongue?
Am I buying a stick to beat myself with
Or contributing to party funds?
Keeping some peasant worker on the poverty line
Picking my coffee beans?
How many innocents lose their lives
In the cost of the packaging?
What am I doing with this blood red bill in my hands?
It's nothing to do with me
I rip it up because I can't pay
And I won't pay
For their mistakes

* * * * * *   *

.19

```
              10
   2     4  9  11
 1    5    12  14
   3 6 7  13 15    21
      8   16 20 22 24
          17 18   23
```

alternative top 50

So we stand accused
Of obeying the rules
Playing it straight, not stepping out of line
Buying into the lies
Slogans and bribes
Cheated out of our hearts, hands and minds
The surplus we made wasted and decayed
Show me the money, I'll show you the crime

We put the work in
We put the time in
Assumed we were
Doing the right thing
We put the effort in
Our whole lives in
But in the end we're second class citizens

So we zipped our lips
We worked for tips
We aimed ever-lower but still missed
In this compassionate land
The helping hand
Shows you two fingers then a fist

We put the work in
We put the time in
What did we get back?
Virtually nothing
We put the effort in
Our whole lives in
But in the end we're second class citizens

No, they don't care
Yes, life's unfair
It's an un-welfare state
We find out too late
Every article of faith requires some proof
It's hard to find a way
Through the bargains on display
To some permanent version of the truth

We put the work in
We put the time in
So why are we just barely surviving?
We put the effort in
Our whole lives in
But in the end we're second class citizens

t v smith

.19

```
      2     4     10
 1        5    9   11
    3   6 7   12  14           25
           8  1315       21
                 16  20  22  24
                   17 18    23
```

62 man down

```
a l t e r n a t i   v e   t o p  50
```

I heard there was a time before my time
When there was no crime
No slums or tower blocks
   Everyone left their doors unlocked
Now I look around and all I see
Is a vision of brutality
Where justice is lost in the edit
Truth's gone as fast as they can shred it
  And if you're down on your luck
    They'll never notice you
Everybody's looking up

 Man down in Martinho
  Man down!
    While all the rest of them
 Were just standing around
  Man down in Martinho
Man down!
I was swallowed by traffic
    No place to turn around

No one's slowing down 'cause that's a lot to ask
When your throat stings and your stomach churns
And the roads are choked with cars
All making last-minute turns
    You can ask
They never answer
Where would they start?
Which piece do you pick up first
    When the whole world's falling apart?
  And in a concrete shanty town
  They'll never pick you up
Everybody walks around
  Man down in Martinho
 Man down!

        You can ask
       They never answer
        At least, not the truth
       You think they do
          But when you're down on your luck
    They never notice you
      They're too busy cleaning up
     Man down in Martinho

Man down!

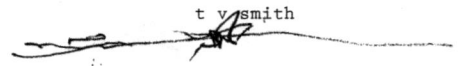

.19

```
              10
    2    4  9  11                    26
 1    5      12  14               25
   3 6 7   13 15          21
        8         16  20  22  24
                 17 18    23
```

alternative top 50

You jumped, you dropped
Your problems got
Difficult to solve
The conservative view
Is that good work shines through
Still the businesses fold
In the money comes
Out the money goes
Charging out of control
It makes you feel so useless
Run rabbit run
You're already half-killing yourself
To get the job done
While they're piling on the pressure
You're missing out on all the fun
Line up with the losers
You feel so useless

If you could have taken your time
You might have got
A different result
Instead of rushing around
Ahead of the crowd
Until you ground to a halt
First you're flying high
Then you're lying low
Buckling under the load
It makes you feel so useless
Run rabbit run
Line up with the losers
You feel so useless

O.K. - you're in business
You've really been set up
When they take away the safety net
You're going to fall the same as all the rest
In the money comes
Out the money goes
Spiralling out of control
It makes you feel so useless

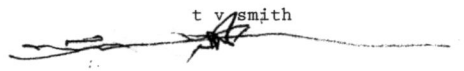

t v smith

.19

27

I 2 4 10 11 26
  3 5 9
    6 7 12 14   25
     8 13 15 21
       16 20 22 24
      17 18   23

66 bored teenagers

alternative top 50

We're talking into corners
　Finding ways to fill the vacuum
　And though our mouths are dry
　We talk in hope to hit on something new
　Tied to the railway tracks
　It's one way to revive but no way to relax

　we talk about the whys and wherefores
　Do we really care at all?
　Talk about the frailty of words
　Is rarely meaningful
　when we're sitting watching the planes
　Burn up through the night like meteorites
　we're just bored teenagers
　Looking for Love
　Or should I say, emotional rages
　Bored teenagers
　Seeing ourselves as Strangers

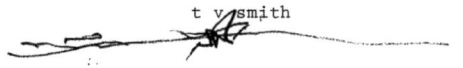

.19

                                    27
                                26
 1 2   4   10 11
    3   5 9   25
       6 7 12 14   21
          8 13 15
              16 20 22 24
                17 18 23
                            28

68 no time to be 21

Life's short
Don't make a mess of it
To the ends of the earth
You'll look for sense in it
No chances, no plans
I'll smash the windows of my box
I'll be a madman
It's no time to be 21
To be anyone

Hold back
See what you miss of it
Out of the shadows
Into the thick of it
No maybes, no guessing
I'm getting wound up
The plot sickens
It's no time to be 21
To be anyone

Strip down
To the bare facts of it
Into the cold heart
No hope and all that shit
No chances, no plans
I think I'll be somebody else
Or else a madman
It's no time to be 21
To be anyone

We'll be your untouchables
We'll be your outcasts
We don't care what you project on us
It's no time to be 21

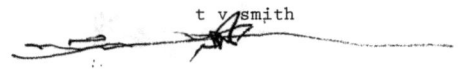
t v smith

.19

```
                                              27
                                           26
 .1  2    4   9 10 11
     3   5      12 14           25
        6 7        13 15    21
           8         16 20 22 24
                   17 18    23
                                           28

                        29
```

70 the future used to be better

alternative top 50

The sights I've seen, the things I've heard
While sliding down the learning curve
Their contract promised me the earth
Through toothy grins and weasel words

With normal jobs and normal lives
They force us to this compromise
Where labour lives and leisure dies
And most of us get by
But I remember the future used to be better

Now voyager, what's left?
You moved so fast you missed the best
And all you got was out of breath
You could call that success
But I remember the future used to be better

Go on, admit it - you know you want to see
All those blank pages in my diary

I'm long on patience, short on cash
My car and my computer crashed
I'm halfway there and halfway back
The world pissed on my purple patch
The light's blocked out, now nothing grows
They've dumbed me down with news and soaps
The end result of all my hopes
Paper cuts from the edge of the envelope
But I remember
When the future used to be better

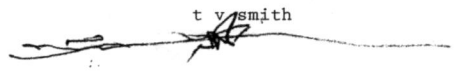
t v smith

.19

```
                              27
  2    4    10                        26
1    5   9    11
   3   6 7  12  14              25
        8  13 15        21
                16  20  22  24
                17  18    23
                                    28

                         29

                       30
```

72 we who wait

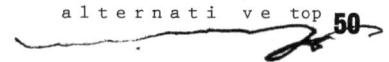

WHO WAIT IN CAFÉ AND MAGAZINE
WHO WAIT FOR MORNING OR FAG MACHINE
WHO LEAVE IT ALL UNFINALISED
AND UNDECIDED
WE WHO WAIT

WHO WAIT IN BUS QUEUE AND PRISON CELL
WHO WAIT FOR ILLNESS TO TAKE ITS TOLL
WHO WAIT FOR GOD KNOWS WHAT
SOMETIMES IT'S NOT CLEAR
TO WE WHO WAIT

I HAVE BEEN DANCING IN THE PENNY ARCADE
I'LL HUG THE SYMBOLS OF MY APATHY
AND HOG THE TASTE OF ANARCHY AND ANIMOSITY
IT'S ANY MEANS OF ESCAPE FOR THOSE OF US WHO WAIT

WHO WAIT IN DRINKING AND LOST CAREER
WHO WAIT FOR LETTER OR HIGH SUMMER
WHO WANT SOME KIND OF CLUE
IT'S NOT JUST TWO PLUS TWO
TO WE WHO WAIT

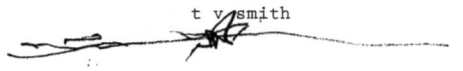
t v smith

.19

                                    27
                                26
 I 2   4   10 11
    3 5 9   12   14   25
     6 7 8   13 15   21
              16 20 22 24
              17 18   23
                                    28

                        29

                    30 31

74 new ways are best

alternative top 50

I'm the original naked man
I get burned to a crisp
Instead of lightly tanned
I don't know what they put
In those aerosol cans
But they tell me that it's for the best
They say you've got to move forward
You've got to change
You can't read a book
Without turning a page
So whatever they offer
You have to take
It's been through every kind of test
And they've proved that
The new ways are best

If things could have been different
They would have been
You can't un-see something
Once it's seen
You can't turn the clock back
Digitally
We follow where others lead
We get the old ingredients, new blend
New packet, same contents
We're told what we want but what do we get?
A new road going where the old one went
We get to fill our time in interesting ways
Jobs pressing buttons eight hours a day
We get to spend more money than we get paid
The good life's here and it won't go away
Nobody move! Nobody think!
According to the latest tests
They've proved that
The new ways are best

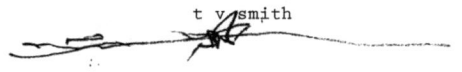

19

```
                                27
                      10                26
  I   2    4    9       11
      3    5                            
          6 7   12  14              25
              8  1315       21
                    16  20  22  24
                      17  18    23
                                        28

                              29


                              30  31


                                    32
```

76   march of the giants

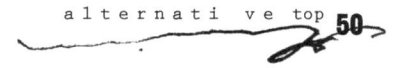

YOU RISE UP OVER THE SKYLINE
PUSHING EVERYTHING OUT OF YOUR WAY
ALL AROUND THE DOGS START HOWLING
AND THE GROUND STARTS TO SWAY
MY HOUSE IS MADE OUT OF MATCHSTICKS
YOUR MAP HAS GOT A BIG 'X' ON
YOU'RE SO BUSY HIKING YOUR EMPIRE UP
YOU'D LET A BABY DROP FROM YOUR ARMS
NO ONE CAN PUT A SPRING IN YOUR STEP
OR THAW YOUR HEART
IT'S NOT ART
IT'S NOT SCIENCE
IT'S A MARCH OF THE GIANTS

I WAKE UP AS THE GREAT LEAP FORWARD
CRASHES DOWN ON MY NEWSPAPER BED
RIGHT NOW I NEED ANOTHER PLACE TO SHOP
LIKE A HOLE IN THE BACK OF MY HEAD
I'LL GET ANOTHER HIGH RISE BLOCK
WHETHER I WANT IT OR NOT
IT'S NOT ART
IT'S NOT SCIENCE
IT'S A MARCH OF THE GIANTS

I'M STAYING SMALL
WHILE YOU GROW STRONG
ON A HUMAN SCALE OF ONE TO TEN
I'M REGISTERING NONE
AND I MAY BE THE FIRST TEST-TUBE ADULT
I DON'T KNOW, I CAN'T HEAR MYSELF THINK
OVER THE CLICK OF THE GEIGER COUNTER
AND THE ROAR OF THE MOTORWAY LINK
THERE'S A THOUSAND HOMELY DREAMS
THAT LIE BENEATH YOUR BULLDOZER, DEAD
WHEN YOU DEMONSTRATE YOUR TALENTS
CLOUDS BLACKEN AND RIVERS RUN RED
WHAT YOU DO FOR AN EXTRA SLICE
OF YOUR DAILY BREAD
IS NOT ART
AND IT'S NOT SCIENCE
IT'S A MARCH OF THE GIANTS
NO ONE CAN LIGHTEN YOUR STEP
OR THAW YOU HEART
IT'S NOT ART
IT'S NOT SCIENCE
IT'S A MARCH OF THE GIANTS

t v smith

                              19

                                        27
                                    26
  1 2   4   10 11
     3 5   9   12 14   25
        6 7   13 15   21
           8   16 20 22 24
                 17 18   23
                                        28

                              29

                          30 31

                                  32

                                    33

78 silicon valley holiday

alternative top 50

You gave them a run for their money
They make you run for your life
You're the beast of burden
Hard working type
In the shipyard
Down the coal mine
You're going on a silicon valley holiday
Hip! Hip! Hooray!
You're going away
On a silicon valley holiday

Far from the pump of the piston
Far from the sweat and grime
Into the new tomorrow
Without a lifeline
Take cover
It's a landslide
And you're going on a silicon valley holiday
Pack your bags right away
Leave now, don't delay
It's a silicon valley holiday

You want to scream, scream
Picture the scene
It's like a bad dream
What happened to your muscle?
You've got your face dirty
And your hands tied
You can clean up
But not on the firm's time
You're going to dive, dive
Below the breadline
And you're going on a silicon valley holiday
Hip! Hip! Hooray!
Despair and dismay
It's a silicon valley holiday

Silicon valley holiday
Bad times are here to stay
You're going away
On a silicon valley holiday

t v smith

.19

```
                                          27
                                  26
 I  2   4    10 11
    3   5   9              
      6 7  12   14             25
         8  13 15       21
              16  20  22  24
                17 18    23
                                  28

                           29              34

                             30  3I


                                      32

                                          33
```

80 thin green line

alternative top 50

We're faced with mile-high piles of money
Sitting in banks
Gold bars, credit cards
Aeroplanes and tanks
Buy, buy, satisfy
Call me when you're rich
Cheap food, cows dying in a ditch
We're having a hard time
Holding the thin green line

We're faced with out-of-town shopping malls
Suburban housing boom
Inner city empty lots
Damp in all the rooms
Bulls, bears, speculators
Marks, Franks, Yen
And the baby's crying again
We're having a hard time
Holding the thin green line

So come on down to the bottle bank
Make your deposit and relax
Nothing's going on behind your back
We'll make all the big decisions
You just watch the television
Smash the brown!
Smash the green!
Smash the clear!
It won't happen here

We watch the last of the species
Vanish from the screens
And get replaced by killer dogs
And their man on the scene
There are peeping toms, pop songs
Crime and sin and sex
All spewing out on newsprint
While the forest dies a death
They're cooling down reactors
While the natives die of thirst
The say let's all pull together
You first!

t v smith

.19

27
          26
 2   4   10
1   3 5 9 11
     6 7 12 14   25
        8 1315   21
            16 20 22 24   35
             17 18 23
                     28

                29   34

                  30 31

                        32

                           33

                              in the arms of my enemy

alternative top 50

I'm free to go where I want
But I walk on razor blades
I'm free to work till I drop
But just for the minimum wage
I watch all the channels
Trying to find my place
Taking every precaution
Still I don't feel safe
Here in the arms of my enemy
I fade away
They're crushing the life right out of me
And there's no escape

I'm like an invalid diva
In need of help
Feel like I'm carrying baggage
I didn't pack myself
Always under surveillance
Even behind closed doors
I must have been brainwashed
To get these dirty thoughts
Here in the arms of my enemy
I suffocate
They're crushing the life right out of me
And there's no escape

My voice never gets heard
Despite my vote
This is the bone of contention
Sticking in my throat
I'd like to say I love you
All I can do is choke
You promised to protect me
That's just a joke
Here in the arms of my enemy
Held on the ropes
They're crushing the life right out of me
And they won't let go

t v smith

```
                    19

                            27
                       26                    36
 1   2    4    10 11
    3    5   9        25
       6 7  12 14
          8 13 15                         35
              16 20 22 24
             17 18  23
                      28

                   29           34

                  30  31


                           32

                              33
```

I see you sparkle in the mud

Like a little diamond in the rough

Ready for the cut, ready for the cut

And you could go either way

Potentially two-faced

Both sides battling for a place

Your glamour fades so quick

Soars up like a rocket

Down like a stick, down like a stick

Be strong when they need it

Be weak when they want it

If you want to fit

84 lion and the lamb

alternative top 50

Stand and say
I am the lion and the lamb
I am part of the plan
I am the lion and the lamb

Now you sparkle in the mud
Diamond in the rough
Ready for the cut
Some stay dull
Some stay blunt
But you will shine up

.19

27
                          26   36
1 2   4   10 11
   3   5 9
      6 7 12 14   25
         8 1315   21
              16 20 22 24   35
              17 18   23
                      28

              29   34

                30 31

                               37
                          32

                          33

new church

alternative top 50

Maybe - maybe a fool for trusting
Maybe - maybe a fool for following
The god of wisdom not of love
But I'm riding with the new church
Relying on the new church
And a new word

Hang on - if you hang on to faith and meekness
Before long, it's power for the strong
It's twisted into something evil, something wrong
So I'm riding with the new church
Relying on the new church
And a new word

So long - goodbye to the blind and the weaklings
Be strong - I'll do what I want
I'll follow my feelings, I'll go where they lead me
I'm riding with the new church
Relying on the new church
And a new word

Strength within you, not without you
The new church needs you

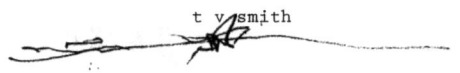

```
                            19

                          27
                        26                36
 2    4    10
1   3   5  9 11
    6 7  12 14        25
       8 1315    21
           16 20 22 24           35
          17 18   23
                        28

                   29           34

                    30 31


                              37
                           32
                                38
                          33
```

88 lord's prayer

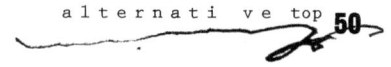

There's no saviour out there
To interfere in your affairs
There ain't no one else who cares
All your good deeds lead nowhere
Life's a crime of passion
Designed for direct action
It's a war so all's fair
This is the Lord's Prayer

Give us the strength of purpose
To reverse all they taught us
Give us the power, give us the wealth
Or else we'll have to help ourselves
I'll recruit a ragged army
To wipe out all who harm me
And I'll be devil-may-care
This is the Lord's Prayer

Back behind the Bible Belt
People scream and people yell
I ain't coming, save yourself!
This is the Lord's Prayer

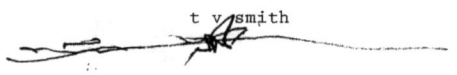

19

27
         26   36
1 2   4   10 11
   3 5 9
     6 7 12 14   25
       8 13 15 21
            16 20 22 24   35
            17 18   23
                  28

29   34

30 31

              37
          32
              38
            33
                39

90 true believers

alternative top 50

Out of town where there's nothing around
Except white puffy clouds
We live on farms, no burglar alarms
Just the sheep, pigs and cows
Forget the losers, we're the producers
And God speeds the plough
Unlike the rest we know we know best
And you'll never change us now, no

We're the true believers
There's a gulf between us
And you'll never reach us
And the dinosaurs, they roam
But the kids are safe at home
And you'll never change that, no

Up in the hills with the suicide pills
We sing around the village pump
Enforce the lesson with a rack full of weapons
And an ammunition dump
Versatile, fertile, give us some dirt
And we'll make the green fields grow
The next generation is ready and waiting
And you'll never change that, no

We're the true believers
There's a world between us
Where temptation leads us
We have no desire to go
Because we walk a narrow road
And you'll never change that, no

Though we're carved from the same flesh
We turned out so different
Now the beaten and the bruised
The morally confused
They're queuing up to invest
As we upset the balance
Between God and Mammon
And advance our own interests, yes

We're the true believers
There's a war between us
For a thousand reasons
Like the oil and guns and gold
And the seeds that can't be sold
By your local farmers, no
We're the true believers
And you'll never change us, no

t v smith

.19

                27
     2   4   10   26   36
 1   5   9   11
    3   6   12   14   25
        7 8 1315   21
              16 20 22 24   35
             17 18   23
                     28

              29   34

              30 31

                    37
              32   40
                    38
              33
                    39

92 xmas bloody xmas

It's been building up
Now we're coming up
To the time of year when greed is good
Snow and icicles
The price triples
But you wouldn't change it if you could

The tills ring out like jingle bells
The kitchen's filled with murderous smells
No-one's going to end up hungry here
We'll snooze under the Xmas tree
While boring films play on T.V.
Forget about reality - cheers!

It's Xmas, Xmas, Xmas bloody Xmas
It's all you ever hear
Xmas, Xmas, Xmas bloody Xmas
Until it almost sounds sincere

Carol singers croon
Sentimental tunes
Suddenly your problems disappear
Am I losing touch
Or did I drink too much
Or is a real solution nowhere near?

This great big party never stops
Hang tinsel round your cardboard box
Last year's leftovers are back in the shops
And landfills spew out plastic bags
From lorryloads of booze and fags
God, don't you hate this time of year?

Under studio lights the Santas fry
In shows recorded last July
Tanned professionals read their lines
To moth-eaten reindeer
Play victim in fake snowball fights
Where no one's injured, no one dies
No one has to sleep outside
Freezing and in fear
Singing, "Goodwill to all mankind!"
We'll put things right some other time
Meanwhile - that special day is here
So happy Xmas, happy bloody Xmas
It almost sounds sincere

t v smith

.19

                                27
                         26   36
  2   4   10
1   3 5   9   11
      6 7 12 14   25
         8 13 15   21
              16 20 22 24   35
               17 18   23
                          28

                    29   34

                       30 31   41

                              37
                          32   40
                              38
                         33
                              39

94 good times are back

alternative top 50

I was trying to remember the good times I've had
Terminally hampered by my short attention span
Were we really so happy? Were the summers so hot?
Were we so young and beautiful? Well, in the end – so what?

I was thinking about my holiday, the one I spent at home
With a vapour trail suntan, depression and a cold
I was hiding from the terrorists, bird flu and SARS
Headline in the paper said, "Water found on Mars!"

I was hanging on the helpline, the hours were crawling past
In a queue of several thousand, somehow still the last
Was it ever better than it is now? I need to know
But all I get is this muzak and a voice that says, "Please hold!"
There's war and the poor, political criminals
No wonder I'm so cynical
Pushed around by bad actors
Feels like we're all going backwards
Come on, get into the action
Stand up now
Catch up now

Perhaps the good times are back
Maybe they never went away
Or never really were so great
Maybe they're just a distraction
From what is actually happening

t v smith

```
                19

                            27
                        26              36
 2    4   10
I   3   5  9 11         
    6 7  12 14      25
       8 1315   21
         16 20 22 24           35
          17 18  23
                   28

                29        34

              30 31          41

                      37      42
                   32     40
                         38
                  33
                            39
```

96   cast of thousands

alternative top 50

You're living in other people's lives
Doesn't seem to be doing you a lot of use
Believing in other people's lies
It's getting pretty hard to tell the truth
When you read the papers
You're being told the easy side of life
Exactly as it appears from the outside
Now you know why the truth comes in disguise
It's the backward slide, so who wants a ride?

When you get to heaven
You'll meet them all again
The cast of thousands
Spouting out of the corporate pen
Demanding your money
To make up something new
Starring new combinations
Of the tried and twisted crew
All the human torches catching fire
Especially for you
The corrupt officials getting caught
Especially for you
The poor and the needy, robbers and killers
Especially for you
Bankrupt stars, competitions, mid-air collisions
Win the home of your dreams!
Rape, runaway wives, other people's lives
Birth, death, money left
Marriage and divorce, suicide
Political intrigues, hospital cases
British weapons to foreign places
Earthquake, flood, bodies in the mud
Poison clouds, a cast of thousands
The gunman opened fire
Especially for you

t v smith

.19

                27
        26   36
   2   4   10
1   5   9 11
  3 6 7 12 14   25
      8 13 15   21
           16 20 22 24   35
          17 18   23
                   28

              29
                        34

           30 3I   4I

                        37   42
                    32   40
                          38   43
                    33
                           39

98 the newshound

alternative top 50

The world loves a story
So I'm on the spot
There are twigs in my hair
I'm completely lost
But somewhere that story
Waits to be found
I'm going to get it
I'm the newshound
You're going to get it
I'm the newshound

I'm on your shoulders
You gladiators
I'm there in the ring
When the lion roars
At outbreaks of wars
I'll be around
Sniffing out a story
I'm the newshound
Lust for glory
I'm the newshound

When you're hungry
Queueing for bread
Or you've been in some accident
And you're wounded
As you regain consciousness
And you look around
Guess who'll you'll see
Yeah - the newshound
Pleased to meet me
I'm the newshound
Here for a reason
You're in season
And I'm the newshound

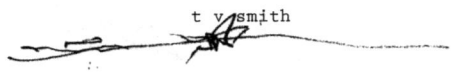

                    19

                              27
                         26   36
  2   4   10 11
1   3 5   9 12 14   25
    6 7 8 1315   21
             16 20 22 24   35
           17 18   23
                         28

                    29
                              34
               30 31   41

                              37   42
                         32   40   44
                              38   43
                    33
                         39

                                        100 television's over

alternative top **50**

Time to pull out the plugs
Have we run out of love?
Have we been deserted
Or let loose?
I've just seen the dead walk by
And they don't seem jealous of my life
Let's take heart, see what lasts
Call it the truth
Television's over

Now we stand on the shore
Now we stand on the edge of some adventure
Now we have to close our eyes
And jump
Now we have no guiding light
And all we see is our own sight
Take heart, take hope
Trust - now
Television's over

Another close-down
Another let down
Another break down
Until I wind down
We're just echoes
We're reflected
Tonight I see the screen
But not the pictures on it

Time to pull out the plugs
Time to look above
Confused by science
Or just confused
Now brave men walk your tube
But tonight they die and that just leaves you
Take heart, see what lasts
Call it Truth
Television's over
Now I feel no hunger
You feel no hunger
We feel no hunger

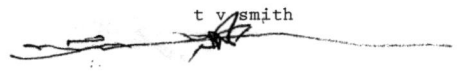

102 coming in to land

alternative top 50

The edge of a revolution
That's exactly where we stand
And though we could seize the moment
We aspire to wear the brand
And we take our place in a profane state
With the common herd, the beautiful, and damned
I've had enough of this grey sky thinking
I'm coming in to land
Crippled by indecision
The chance slips from our hands
I put in a call for guidance
But the frequency was jammed
Feel like I lost my way in a bad screenplay
The jokes are old and the laughter's only canned
I've been circling round for too long now
I'm coming in to land
So we head for annihilation
And the route's already planned
It's a lesson in subjugation
But the malls are always crammed
I drift up here in this atmosphere
So thin that I can barely even stand
I'll be leaving this lazy orbit soon
I'm coming in to land
Clear the runway
I'm coming in to land

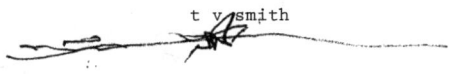
t v smith

.19

27
26   36
1 2 4 10 11
 3 5 9   25
  6 7 12 14   35
   8 13 15   21
      16 20 22 24
      17 18 23
             28

29   34

30 31   41

         37   42
    32   40
              43   44
         38
     33
          39

4

45

104 borderline

alternative top 50

Things bad and getting worse
All stations on red alert
That black hole could swallow you
It's not just you
Sometimes I feel it too

Too many silly rules to hold
She's unstable - she's gonna blow!
Barbarians are breaking through
It's not just you
Sometime I feel it too
On the borderline
Why don't you get on my side
On the borderline
We could save each other's lives

Exercise your secret strength
You don't have to run
You don't have to hide
You can do what you like
Look your enemy right in the eyes
And say, stay away
Because I keep my monsters tied
On the borderline
Where the rules do not apply
On the borderline
You'd better steer wide
On the borderline
There's still something pure that's mine
On the borderline

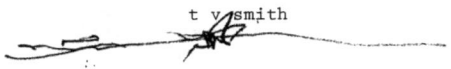

19

27
26   36
2   4   10 11
1   9   25
  3 5   12 14   35
   6 7   13 15   21
      8   16 20 22 24
            17 18   23
                     28

29   34

30 31   41

          37   42
      32   40
              38   43   44
      33
              39

4

45

106 statute of liberty

alternative top 50

REBELS AND RANTERS
HOLDERS OF BANNERS
ANARCHISTS, ACID-HEADS
STREET MARCHERS, STAY-IN-BEDS
SOMETIMES YOUR PROTEST
JUST WON'T GET NOTICED
DEPENDS ON TIMING
WHOSE STAR IS RISING
WHAT STORY'S IN THE NEWS
WHICH WAY THEY PITCH THE TRUTH
WHICH WAY THEY SHAKE IT
SUBVERT AND SHAPE IT
SO THEY CAN MAKE IT PAY
BUT YOU CAN STAND FREE
UNDER THE STATUTE OF LIBERTY
JUST KEEP ON PUSHING THEM AWAY

MEDIA OUTCRIES
SKETCHES AND OUTLINES
THEY'RE IRRESISTIBLE
ONE SOUND-BITE AND YOU'RE FULL
COLUMNS AND LEADERS
MARCH THROUGH THEIR READERS
UNTIL THEY ALL THINK THE SAME
BUT YOU CAN STAND FREE
UNDER THE STATUTE OF LIBERTY
JUST KEEP ON PUSHING THEM AWAY

WHO AIRS THE VOICES?
PROVIDES THE CHOICES
OF WHICH INTEREST TO PROTECT?
GAGS SOME AND NOT THE REST?
FREE SPEECH CAN SCRAMBLE
WORDS ARE A GAMBLE

HAPPENS SO OFTEN
AND TO SO MANY
FIRST THEY'RE THE COMING STORM
THEN THEY'RE THE UNIFORM
THEN THEY DESERT YOU
HARASS AND HURT YOU
UNTIL YOU DO WHAT THEY SAY
BUT YOU CAN STAND FREE
UNDER THE STATUTE OF LIBERTY
JUST KEEP ON
PUSHING THEM AWAY

t v smith

48

19

27

2 10 26 36

1 4 11 9

3 5

12 14 25

6 7

13 15 21

8

16 20 22 24 35

18 23

17

28

29 34

30 31 41

42

37

40 44

32

43

38

33

39

4

45

alternative top 50

It's not life
It's just a short stretch of time
A lesson you have to sit through
You gambled and lost
Here's the cost
Three months of Sundays staring at you
Count one for the dirty deed
Two for the need
That wounds you like a poison arrow
Three for the living rough
And the fact that times are tough
That drove you off the straight and narrow

Small turns to big
When a joker in a wig
Looks down at you pure as the driven snow
In a back room with a drink
He doesn't think
Of the years that tumble down like dominoes
Count one for the dirty deed
Two for the need
That wounds you like a poison arrow
Three for the shame
You can never clear your name
Or get back on the straight and narrow

And it feels like
Big fists keep punching you down
And while the world's spinning round
You're counted out
One for the dirty deed
Two for the need
That wounds you like a poison arrow
The wages of sin
Are a pattern that sets in
And keeps you off the straight and narrow
So many mouths to feed
You look at all that greed
It chills you to the marrow
Three! says the judge
And reinforces a grudge
And keeps you off the straight and narrow

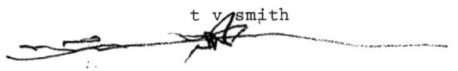
t v smith

        4⁸

    19

          27
                  26   36
I 2   4   10 11
   3 5 9   12   14   25
    6 7   13 15   21
       8   16 20 22 24   35
          17 18   23
                      28

        29   34

      30 31   41

                 37   42
              32   40   44
                  38   43
           33
              39

                              4

                         45

110 gary gilmore's eyes

alternative top **50**

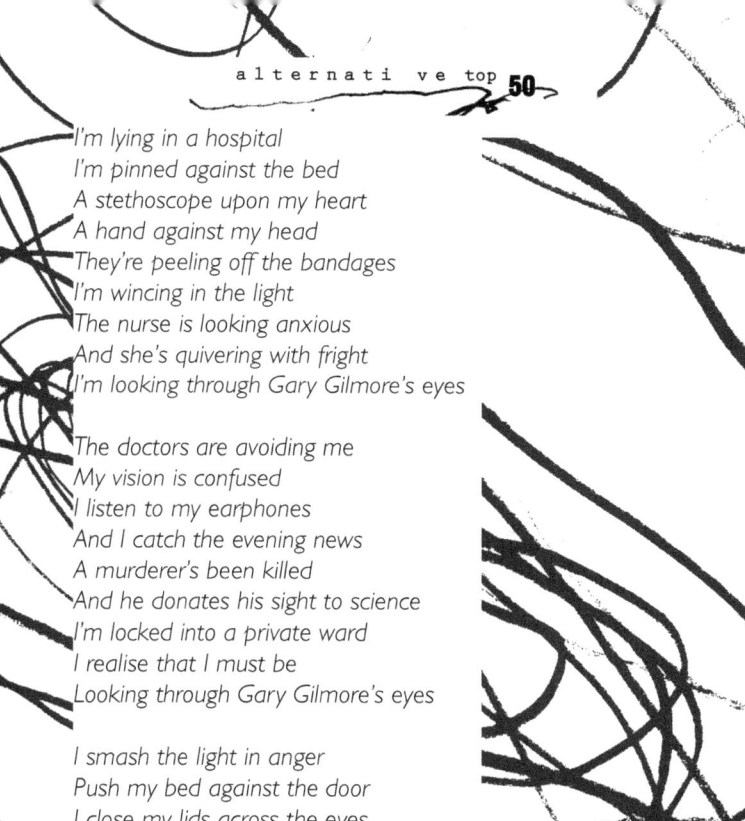

I'm lying in a hospital
I'm pinned against the bed
A stethoscope upon my heart
A hand against my head
They're peeling off the bandages
I'm wincing in the light
The nurse is looking anxious
And she's quivering with fright
I'm looking through Gary Gilmore's eyes

The doctors are avoiding me
My vision is confused
I listen to my earphones
And I catch the evening news
A murderer's been killed
And he donates his sight to science
I'm locked into a private ward
I realise that I must be
Looking through Gary Gilmore's eyes

I smash the light in anger
Push my bed against the door
I close my lids across the eyes
And wish to see no more
The eye receives the messages
And sends them to the brain
No guarantee the stimuli
Must be perceived the same when
Looking through Gary Gilmore's eyes

Gary don't need his eyes to see
Gary and his eyes have parted company

t v smith

                                                                    48

                              19

                                      27

                              26   36
1   2   4   10 11
    3 5   9
      6 7 12 14   25
          8 13 15   35
                16 20 21 22 24
                 17 18   23
                             28

                         29   34

                            30 31   41

                                        37   42
                                    40   44
                              32   43
                                     38
                                33
                                      39

                                                              46

                                                         45

                                                         50

112 i will walk you home

alternative top 50

I will walk you home
   I'll make sure you're never alone
   I will stay by your side
   Until we reach
Your door

   Before you start
    Wondering what your heart
    Really fell for

Before you start thinking
  And thinking and thinking
    And thinking once more

                                       I will walk you home

www.ingramcontent.com/pod-product-compliance
Lightning Source LLC
Chambersburg PA
CBHW071232090426
42736CB00014B/3051